STRESSMASTER INTERNATIONAL

How frequently do you (Circle the Number)...

		VERY RARELY				VERY FREQUENTLY
21.	Move, walk, or eat rapidly?	1	2	3	4	5
22.	Have moist palms, feet, or underarms?	1	2	3	4	5
23.	Have very little time to relax and let go?	1	2	3	4	5
24.	Feel unenthusiastic?	1	2	3	4	5
25.	Overwork a task to get it perfect?	1	2	3	4	5
26.	Get upset when a joke is made about you?	1	2	3	4	5
27.	Feel unhappy?	1	2	3	4	5
28.	Demonstrate that you are a perfectionist at what you do?	1	2	3	4	5
29.	Over perspire?	1	2	3	4	5
30.	Find it difficult to slow down?	1	2	3	4	5
31.	Feel pessimistic?	1	2	3	4	5
32.	Hurry the speech of others by saying such things as: "uh-huh" or "yes, yes, yes"?	1	2	3	4	5
33.	Fail to delegate because you believe you can do it better than others?	1	2	3	4	5
34.	Feel discouraged?	1	2	3	4	5
35.	Talk about people who disappoint you?	1	2	3	4	5
36.	Find that you are unable to locate things such as papers, tools, folders?	1	2	3	4	5
37.	Have difficulty falling or staying asleep?	1	2	3	4	5
38.	Feel unappreciated?	1	2	3	4	5
39.	Have cold hands or feet?	1	2	3	4	5
40.	Talk rapidly?	1	2	3	4	5
41.	Feel frustrated at others' behaviors (e.g., become irritated at your progress behind a slow driver or in a line of customers waiting to be served)?	1	2	3	4	5

© 2014 James C. Petersen, Ph.D. All rights reserved.

STRESSMASTER INTERNATIONAL

LE - LIFE EVENTS

Check each of the following that have happened to you during the past twelve (12) months.

42. ___	Death of a spouse or loved one	100 pts	_____
43. ___	Divorce or marital separation	85 pts	_____
44. ___	Arrest or jail term	80 pts	_____
45. ___	Death of a family member or close friend	75 pts	_____
46. ___	Injury or illness to you	70 pts	_____
47. ___	Major marital or family conflicts	70 pts	_____
48. ___	Loss of a job or unemployment (quit or fired)	65 pts	_____
49. ___	Retirement	60 pts	_____
50. ___	Major injury or illness of family member	50 pts	_____
51. ___	Pregnancy or addition of family member	50 pts	_____
52. ___	Financial loss or difficulties	50 pts	_____
53. ___	Victim of a crime	45 pts	_____
54. ___	Change of residence	40 pts	_____
55. ___	Involved in a law suit	40 pts	_____
56. ___	Sexual harassment	40 pts	_____

Total points above and enter in this box.   LE = [   ]

HA - HASSLES

Check each of the following that have happened to you during the past three (3) mo.

57. ___ Challenge of a new career (reentry career)	68. ___ Misplaced or lost things
58. ___ Concern about weight/health	69. ___ Felt lonely
59. ___ Not enough money for basics	70. ___ Too many responsibilities
60. ___ Not enough rest or sleep	71. ___ Problems with children
61. ___ Conflicts with spouse or close friend	72. ___ Being a single parent
62. ___ Difficulties with employees or friends	73. ___ Household repairs
63. ___ Difficulties with boss or supervisor	74. ___ Cared for aging parents
64. ___ Difficulties balancing home or work life	75. ___ Delayed in heavy traffic
65. ___ Concerned about meeting high standards	76. ___ People making life difficult
66. ___ Problems getting along with coworkers	77. ___ Automobile repairs
67. ___ Not enough money for social activities	78. ___ Wasted time

Total points above and enter in this box.   HA = [   ]

www.STRESSMASTER.com

STRESSMASTER INTERNATIONAL

ABOUT THE SMQ - CHURCH MINISTRY VERSION

OVERVIEW

- **TAKING THE SMQ (P - 2)**
  In this section, you will answer 87 research based questions about stress and you.

- **SCORING THE SMQ (P - 6)**
  Next, you will score the SMQ and, if available, your Companion's SMQ.

- **YOUR STRESS PROFILE (P - 8)**
  At this point you will graph and view your scores on 11 stress "risk" scales.

- **STRESSMASTERY GUIDE (P - 12)**
  Based upon your "risk" scores, you will be provided with the Stressmastery Guide to assist you in the interpreting your results.

- **ACTION PLAN (P -44)**
  Knowledge without a plan does create change. Here you will create an Action Plan based upon what you identified as the key areas on which to focus.

- **CONTRACT FOR CHANGE (P - 27)**
  To help you make changes, you will be provided with Contract for Change that will enable you to make a commitment to becoming stress resilient and psychologically hardy!

- **FINDING RESOURCES (P - 48)**
  Last, you will be provided with a list of resources to use as needed to stay on the path of stress mastery.

Welcome to the Stress Management Questionnaire Church Ministry Version (SMQ-CMV). Over the past 30 years, through scientific research and use by trainers, consultants and mental health professionals worldwide, the SMQ has become one of the few valid and effective stress self-assessment and educational tools available. Now, with the help of the Reverend Paul Bailey, MA, we have integrated Biblical principles and scripture with evidenced-based techniques and concepts to provide a tool that can be used to help reduce stress, increase mental and physical hardiness and begin the "walk" of becoming more stress resilient.

The SMQ is a personal stress-assessment tool that provides solid information about you, the nature of stress and how stress may be affecting you at this time in your life. The SMQ can be used as your personal self-improvement program or as part of a broader stress management program and is appropriate for the clergy, lay professionals and parishioners alike.

HOW TO TAKE THE SMQ

Taking the SMQ-CMV is easy. Simply answer 87 questions that follow as honestly as possible. Since you're taking this to learn about yourself, honesty is the best policy! Your first reaction is usually the best. After completing the SMQ, you will add up your scores for each of the 11 stress "risk" scales. Then, you will profile your results on a chart that compares your scores on each scale to the norm group. A "risk" level for each scale will be provided for your consideration.

THE STRESSMASTERY GUIDE

Once you have your scores and know your stress "risk" level, you will be provided with the Stressmastery Guide to aide you in understanding the meaning of each scale along with WHAT TO KNOW and WHAT TO DO if you scored HIGH on any of the scales.

The Stressmastery Guide provides proven effective information, tools and techniques to help you to master your own personal stress. Given the information provided by the SMQ, perhaps facilitated by a minister or pastor, professional coach or participation in a stress management program, you will become better equipped to improve the way you respond to life's stressors and live a life of stress resilience and stress mastery!

"Learn to Thrive, Not Just Survive...
In A World Of Stress"
Stressmaster

© 2014 James C. Petersen, Ph.D. All rights reserved.

STRESSMASTER INTERNATIONAL
STRESS MANAGEMENT QUESTIONNAIRE (SMQ)

Please answer the following questions about yourself in terms of the last few months.

How frequently do you (Circle the Number)...

		VERY RARELY				VERY FREQUENTLY
1.	Become impatient when performing repetitious acts (e.g., filling out bank deposit slips, writing checks, washing dishes, etc.)?	1	2	3	4	5
2.	Dwell on the incompetencies of others who stand in the way of your progress?	1	2	3	4	5
3.	Notice that you have a fast pulse?	1	2	3	4	5
4.	Not accomplish what you set out to do?	1	2	3	4	5
5.	Have asthma or hay fever flare-ups?	1	2	3	4	5
6.	Insist upon no mistakes from your subordinates or those around you?	1	2	3	4	5
7.	Take time to do something that you really enjoy?	1	2	3	4	5
8.	Have indigestion?	1	2	3	4	5
9.	Feel impatient at the rate at which events take place?	1	2	3	4	5
10.	Feel sad?	1	2	3	4	5
11.	Take quick, short, or no breaks during the day?	1	2	3	4	5
12.	Have shortness of breath?	1	2	3	4	5
13.	Think about getting out of your job or life situation?	1	2	3	4	5
14.	Have headaches?	1	2	3	4	5
15.	Take more time than usual to do things?	1	2	3	4	5
16.	Have constipation/diarrhea?	1	2	3	4	5
17.	Become irritated with the mistakes of others?	1	2	3	4	5
18.	In a competitive situation tend to become upset or angry if you are not the best?	1	2	3	4	5
19.	Avoid tasks and responsibilities?	1	2	3	4	5
20.	Think that what you do is rather pointless?	1	2	3	4	5

LW - LIFE/WORK SATISFACTION

How satisfied are you with your*...

		VERY SATISFIED				VERY UNSATISFIED
79.	Career choice?	1	2	3	4	5
80.	Job choice?	1	2	3	4	5
81.	Coworkers?	1	2	3	4	5
82.	Level of income?	1	2	3	4	5
83.	Immediate supervisor?**	1	2	3	4	5
84.	Amount of work?	1	2	3	4	5
85.	Advancement opportunities?	1	2	3	4	5
86.	Personal relationships?	1	2	3	4	5
87.	Level of exercise/personal fitness?	1	2	3	4	5

Total CIRCLED numbers and enter in this box. LW =

* If you are a homemaker, answer in terms of your work /career as a homemaker, mother, father, etc.

** If you do not report to anyone but yourself, answer in terms of your level of satisfaction with your "self management" with your personal life or work activities.

STRESSMASTER INTERNATIONAL
SCORING THE SMQ

SCORING YOUR SMQ - Participant Form

For <u>each scale below</u>, enter your responses (1,2,3,4 or 5) from questions 1-41 (pp. 2-3) on the line provided. Add the numbers and put the total in the Score Box to the right. This is your score for each scale.

SMQ SCALE							YOUR SCORE
HO	QUESTION #	1	2	9	18	41	
PE	QUESTION #	6	17	25	28	33	
TI	QUESTION #	21	32	40			
DI	QUESTION #	13	34	35	38		
BR	QUESTION #	10	24	26	27	31	
UA	QUESTION #	4	15	19	20	36	
TE	QUESTION #	7	11	23	30		
PS	QUESTION #	3	5	8	12	14	Continue on next line
	QUESTION #	16	22	29	37	39	

LW For the LW - LIFE/WORK SATISFACTION SCALE, enter the total from page 5.

LE For the LE - LIFE EVENTS SCALE, enter the total from page 4.

HA For the HA - HASSLES SCALE, enter the total from page 4.

SCORING THE SMQ - Companion Form

As with scoring your SMQ, follow the same procedure with the Companion Form data. Note: if your companion selected Do Not Know, <u>enter the score you gave for that question on your SMQ</u>. If you do not have a <u>completed</u> Companion Form, you may skip this section. If you get a completed Companion Form later, simply fill out this section when you have time.

SMQ SCALE							YOUR SCORE
HO	QUESTION #	1	2	9	18	41	☐
PE	QUESTION #	6	17	25	28	33	☐
TI	QUESTION #	21	32	40			☐
DI	QUESTION #	13	34	35	38		☐
BR	QUESTION #	10	24	26	27	31	☐
UA	QUESTION #	4	15	19	20	36	☐
TE	QUESTION #	7	11	23	30		☐
PS	QUESTION #	3	5	8	12	14	☐
	QUESTION #	16	22	29	37	39	☐

LW   For the LW - LIFE/WORK SATISFACTION SCALE, enter the total from page 4 of the Companion's Questionnaire. ☐

LE   For the LE - LIFE EVENTS SCALE, enter the total from page 3 of the Companion's Questionnaire. ☐

HA   For the HA - HASSLES SCALE, enter the total from page 3 of the Companion's Questionnaire. ☐

STRESSMASTER INTERNATIONAL
YOUR STRESS RISK PROFILE

INSTRUCTIONS

Transfer the scores from your SMQ (page 6) and your Companion's SMQ (page 7, if available) in the boxes below. On Graph I place a dot (•) on the line corresponding to each of your scale score. Then, place another dot (•) on the line corresponding to each of your companion's scores. Draw lines between the dots on each scale to show your profile. Do this for both you and your companion's scores. Use different color pens to show the difference between your view of yourself and your companion's view.

Place your scores and your companion scores in the boxes below . . .

	HO	PE	TI	DI	BR	UA	TE
YOUR SMQ	☐	☐	☐	☐	☐	☐	☐
COMPANION SMQ	☐	☐	☐	☐	☐	☐	☐

GRAPH I

7 STRESS WARNING SIGNS — RISK LEVEL

T-Scores across scales HO, PE, TI, DI, BR, UA, TE:

T-Score	HO	PE	TI	DI	BR	UA	TE	Risk Level
80								HIGH
75		25			25	25	20	HIGH
70	25		15	20				HIGH
65		20		16		20		HIGH
60	20		12		20		16	MEDIUM
55				12		15		MEDIUM
50	15	15	9					MEDIUM
45				8	15	10	12	MEDIUM
40		10	6					MEDIUM
35	10			4		5		LOW
30		5	3		10		8	LOW
25	5							LOW
20					5		4	LOW

www.STRESSMASTER.com

STRESSMASTER INTERNATIONAL

CONTINUE THE PROCESS FOR GRAPH II AND GRAPH III

As you did for Graph I, transfer the scores for the following scales into the boxes and then plot the results on the appropriate line for each scale. If you do not have your Companion Form data, then only place your scores in the boxes below at this time. You can go back later and add your companion scores when it becomes available.

Place your scores and your companion scores in the boxes below . . .

	PS	LW	LE	HA
YOUR SMQ	☐	☐	☐	☐
COMPANION SMQ	☐	☐	☐	☐

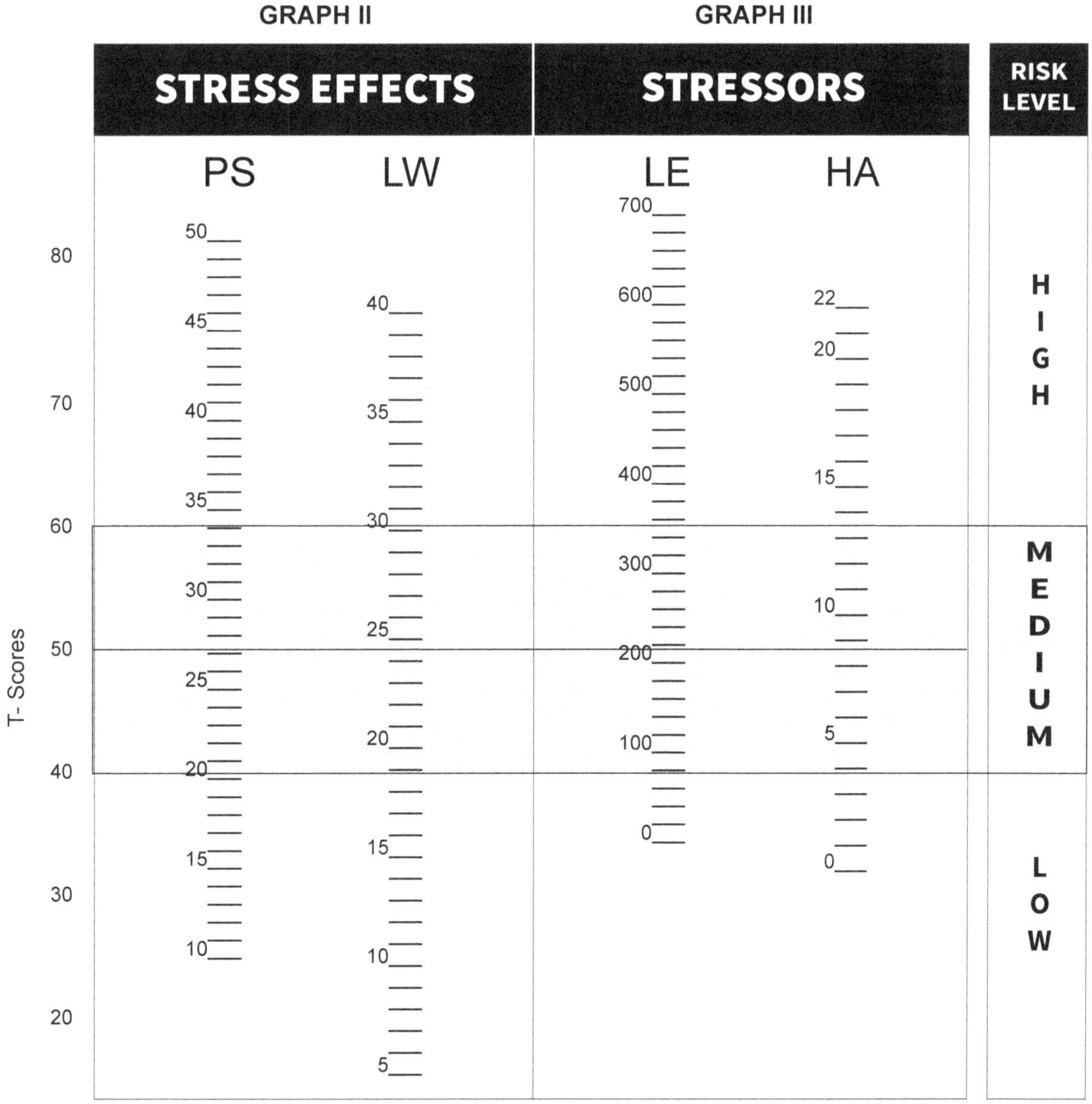

GRAPH II — STRESS EFFECTS (PS, LW)

GRAPH III — STRESSORS (LE, HA)

RISK LEVEL: HIGH / MEDIUM / LOW

(T-Scores axis: 20–80; PS scale 10–50; LW scale 5–40; LE scale 0–700; HA scale 0–22)

STRESSMASTER INTERNATIONAL
STRESSMASTERY GUIDE FOR MINISTERS AND THEIR CHURCHES

"I do not pray for a lighter load, but for a stronger back."
Phillips Brooks

No matter how noble the work, how high the calling, how large or small the church, there are no stress-free leadership positions, or stress-free lives for Christians. EVERYBODY HAS STRESS!

JESUS - John 16:33 (NIV) 33
"I have told you these things, so that in me you may have peace.
In this world you will have trouble. But take heart! I have overcome the world."

Job 5:7 (NIV)
"Yet man is born to trouble as surely as sparks fly upward."

All through the scriptures we find spiritual leaders and followers of Christ dealing with stress. When there were multiple stressors and highly stressful circumstances or demands the impact was rarely healthy. The outcomes often caused them to have misplaced priorities, lose focus, make bad decisions, and in extreme cases, limited or minimized their effectiveness for the work of God.

2 Timothy 4:5 (NLT)
But you should keep a clear mind in every situation. Don't be afraid of suffering for the Lord. Work at telling others the Good News, and fully carry out the ministry God has given you.

This verse highlights some of the impacts of stress. It is very difficult to keep a clear mind that is sharp and focused in order to make the best decisions possible and provide solid leadership when experiencing high levels of stress. It is also challenging, if not impossible, to FULLY carry out the responsibilities of church ministry and leadership when stress is burning up so much of your emotional energy.

STRESSMASTER INTERNATIONAL

THE IMPORTANCE OF STRESS RESILIENCE FOR PASTORS & PEOPLE

Why it is important for the church to put more effort into helping people and pastors deal with stress*...

- 1500 pastors leave the ministry each month due to moral failure, spiritual burnout, or contention in their churches.
- 90% of pastors stated they are frequently fatigued, and worn out on a weekly and even daily basis
- 80% of pastors feel unqualified and discouraged in their role as pastor.
- 80% of seminary & Bible school graduates who enter the ministry will leave the ministry within the first 5 years.
- 75% of ministers are extremely or highly stressed
- 70% of pastors constantly fight depression.
- 70% said the only time they spend studying the Word is when they are preparing their sermons (This is Key).
- 50% of pastors' marriages will end in divorce.
- 50% of pastors are so discouraged that they would leave the ministry if they could, but have no other way of making a living. (over 70% consider it on a regular basis)
- Almost 40% polled said they have had an extra-marital affair since beginning their ministry.
- 23% of the pastors we surveyed said they felt happy and content on a regular basis with who they are in Christ, in their church, and in their home

It is our desire that the tools contained within the Stress Master program will be used to equip church leaders and congregants get stress under control so the word of Psalms 119:143 can be theirs.

Psalms 119:143 (NLT)
"As pressure and stress bear down on me, I find joy in your commands."

Proverbs 3:5-6 (NIV)
The pathway to mastering stress..."Trust in the Lord with all your heart and lean not on your own understanding; in all your ways submit to him, and he will make your paths straight.

*(Survey conducted by Barna Research Institute of 1050 pastors at two separate pastors conferences.)

The **Stressmastery Guide for Ministers and Their Churches** provides biblical and secular information on the meaning of each Stress Management Questionnaire (SMQ) scale along with **WHAT TO KNOW** and **WHAT TO DO** if you scored high on any given scale.

The SMQ is both a personal stress "risk" assessment and an educational tool that can help you to identify and understand your Stress Warning Signs, types of Stressors you are currently facing and the possible Effects of Stress on your health and well being. The SMQ is comprised of 11 scales in three (3) separate stress categories; they are:

I - STRESS WARNING SIGNS SCALES

The Stress Warning Signs Scales are the result of a validation study conducted funded by the National Institute of Occupational Safety and Health (Petersen, J. and Lawrence, H. NIOSH, 1982). The specific scales are:

Hostility/Anger (HO)
Perfectionism (PE)
Time-Urgency (TI)
Disappointment (DI)
Burnout (BR)
Underachievement (UA)
Tension (TE)

II - STRESS EFFECTS SCALES

The Stress Effects Scales shows how stress may be affecting you at both a physical and emotional level. The two scales are:

Physical Stress Effects (PE)
Life Work Satisfaction (LW)

III - STRESSOR SCALES

The Stressor Scales reflect the two major types of stressors that are known to be a cause or "trigger" of the stress response. The two scales are:

Life Events (LE)
Hassles (HA)

STRESSMASTER INTERNATIONAL

Each SMQ Scale provides a view of one important aspect of stress and how it may be affecting you at this time. Your "Risk Level" relates to the "risk" of having or developing specific stress-related physical, behavioral or emotional problems. Having a high score on any given scale only indicates that you may be at "risk" of developing stress related problems, but it does not mean you will necessarily experience any problems.

Based on your responses to the 87 SMQ questions, you were placed in a **High, Medium-High, Medium, Medium-Low** or **Low "Risk"** area for each of the scales. Research shows that high scores on one or more of the Seven Stress Warning Sign Scales are associated with such physical problems as: headaches, cardiovascular disease, bowel disturbances, or emotional issues like burnout or excessive tension.

A **High Score** on any of the SMQ scales is a warning to look more closely to determine what you can do to reduce or change your level of stress. A high score on more than one of the Seven Stress Warning Sign Scales puts you at greater risk of developing stress-related problems. Again, everyone is different so use this information to see if stress is causing you physical or emotional problems.

A **Medium to Medium High Score** on any of the SMQ scales places you in a borderline situation. Check to see if stress is becoming a problem for you now. Determine if you could do more to improve your response to life's stressors and daily hassles. If you have a positive attitude, feel in control of your life and have few health issues, you probably have little "risk". However, if you feel that things are not improving in your life or work, experience more stress than usual or you do not feel in control of important situations, then begin to apply some of the techniques shared in the STRESSMASTER GUIDE.

If your scores fall into the **Medium to Low "Risk"** area, chances are you are doing better than most people. Keep up the good work. However, always be on guard for the encroachment of stressors in your life and a deterioration of how well you are mastering those stressors.

Disclaimer:
Regardless of your scores, if you are in acute distress or feel that life is hopeless, seek out a competent mental health professional immediately. This GUIDE is not intended to replace good quality medical and psychological assistance. If you need help, seek it out today! .

*This GUIDE may be produced **only one time** by the person who has taken the Online SMQ.*
Do not duplicate, copy or disseminate in any form without written permission from Dr. James Petersen.

STRESSMASTER is an international stress management consulting, training, and publishing company headquartered in Phoenix, AZ.

STRESSMASTER INTERNATIONAL
STRESS WARNING SIGNS

AREA I
Seven Stress Warning Signs

How did you do on the SMQ? Place an (X) in the space below that corresponds to your "Risk" score obtained from your SMQ results. The SMQ will guide you in identifying your stress "warning" signs and in discovering new and more effective ways to master stress. The 7 scales that make up the Stress Warning Signs are:

RISK LEVEL

	Low	Medium-Low	Medium	Medium-High	High
Hostility/Anger (HO)	_____	_____	_____	_____	_____
Perfectionism (PE)	_____	_____	_____	_____	_____
Time Urgency (TE)	_____	_____	_____	_____	_____
Disappointment (DI)	_____	_____	_____	_____	_____
Burnout (BR)	_____	_____	_____	_____	_____
Underachievement (UA)	_____	_____	_____	_____	_____
Tension (TE)	_____	_____	_____	_____	_____

Comments/Notes: What are your "warning" signs?

HOSTILITY/ANGER SCALE (HO)

YOUR RISK LEVEL _____

The research on anger and stress is widely studied and the research is clear...anger is <u>the number one behavioral factor most highly correlated</u> with an increased risk of coronary heart stroke, myocardial infarction and high blood pressure. Other physical and behavioral stress problems are also known to be directly influenced by stress. For example, gastrointestinal or stomach problems have a high correlation with anger. The Hostility/Anger Scale (HO) scale assesses the degree to which you are experiencing frustration and anger at this time.

WHAT TO KNOW

(Ephesians 4:26-27, 29 & 31)
"In your anger do not sin" Do not let the sun go down while you are still angry, and do not give the devil a foothold... Do not let any unwholesome talk come out of your mouths, but only what is helpful for building others up according to their needs, that it may benefit those who listen...Get rid of all bitterness, rage and anger, brawling and slander, along with every form of malice.

A high level of anger is a strong behavioral predictor of early illness and, possibly, even death. This scale measures such things as irritability, anger, and impatience and is also one of the classic Type-A behaviors. If you scored <u>medium to high</u> on this scale, it may be wise to find more constructive and appropriate ways of dealing with your angry thoughts and, ultimately, how you treat others.

Most anger is harmful and counterproductive; it undermines relationships and can result in both physical and emotional scars. Anger is most often expressed in the form of verbal abuse, such as the "putting-down" or yelling at a child, spouse or, even, a coworker when they do not meet your expectations or needs.

Anger is an attempt to control the actions, thoughts and feelings of others through coercion and force. People often use anger as an emotional hammer to get what they want. While anger can be expressed directly by "lashing out," it can also be shown indirectly through "passive-aggressive" behavior. With passive-aggressive behavior, individuals punish others by being belligerent, not responding, pouting or simply running away. This is emotional bondage that is, unfortunately, often very effective at controlling others.

Determine if the anger you feel is excessive or harmful to you or those around you. If anger has affected you and, possibly, your loved ones or friends, consider developing new ways of thinking and treating others.

WHAT TO DO

There are many ways to control anger. The key is to change your thoughts about the person or situation. When anger erupts, the first step is to recognize that you are, in fact, angry. Knowing that you are in an agitated "angry state" and possibly not in control of your words or actions, means it is time to STOP, THINK and RELAX. Force yourself to recognize there is a better way to deal with people who fail to meet your expectations.

FEAR DRIVES ANGER

Since fear is the engine that drives people to do such offensive things such as hit, yell or scream at someone, ask yourself, "What am I afraid of right now?" Chances are you are experiencing anxiety and fear that the person will not do what you want? You may feel anxious when you're not in control and respond accordingly?

If anger is a challenge for you, recognize that the need to control others is often unrealistic and counter-productive. If anxiety about a situation or person is high, work to change or modify your thinking about that individual. Once you do, you will be able to master your fear more effectively and your response to the stressor that irritates you will be much more appropriate and effective.

Philippians 4:8 (NIV)
"Finally, brothers and sisters, whatever is true, whatever is noble, whatever is right, whatever is pure, whatever is lovely, whatever is admirable—if anything is excellent or praiseworthy—think about such things.

PRACTICE "LETTING GO"

Proverbs 15:1 (NIV)
"A gentle answer turns away wrath, but a harsh word stirs up anger."

"Letting go" is the key to freeing yourself from excessive anger. Our culture teaches us to always take action and maintain control. While this approach is good in some situations, it is harmful when there is no real threat. By "letting go," you will actually gain control over yourself. And, when you do become aware of any excessive anger, aggression or hostility toward others, you can begin to talk to yourself in a new and more effective way.

Flow! Don't try to control fear, flow with it. The more you focus on fear...the more you get. Once you have recognized the fear behind anger, you can give yourself permission to let it go. Doing so will allow the fear to flow through and then out of you. Energy is wasted trying to push away from our fears. Unfortunately, this keeps us in the middle of our fear and anxiety. Accept that the feared condition has occurred and take positive steps to change or make the best of the situation.

WORK ON SELF-ESTEEM

Most people experience some frustration and anger from time to time. It's normal. However, a positive and productive expression of that anger is essential. A good sense of self-esteem will enable you to express anger and frustration in a more effective way.

When self-esteem improves, it is possible to accept others for who they are and to resist the use of anger as a way to get your way. For example, you might say to yourself:

**"I can let go and it's OK.
Letting go does not mean I'm out of control."**

"I can let go and still feel 'in control."

"Letting go makes me feel better. That will make the situation better."

"I don't need anger to change this person or situation at this time."

"Anger is not controlling me, I can control my anger."

"I am not an angry person. ANGER is destructive. I will raise myself above this anger and LET GO."

BE PREPARED FOR ANGER

James 1:19 (NIV)
"My dear brothers and sisters, take note of this: Everyone should be quick to listen, slow to speak and slow to become angry, because human anger does not produce the righteousness that God desires."

Be prepared for anger to happen. Think about when you get angry. Who do you get angry with and why? Write down or make a mental note of when you feel anger or express it either outwardly toward others or inwardly toward yourself. By becoming aware of the circumstances that trigger anger you will be better prepared to STOP ANGER in its tracks.

Re-think how you will respond differently when others do not live up to your expectations. You may not always succeed, but if you make the effort you will make progress. Look for small successes and reward yourself for progress.

USE "I-MESSAGES"

"I-Messages" are effective ways to communicate with others and can defuse a potentially explosive situation. Use "I-Messages" as an alternatives to yelling. "I-Messages" means telling the person <u>how you feel</u> because of what they did or did not do. "I-Messages" focus on behavior, not the person as a human being. For example, a common anger expression might be: "You idiot! Where have you been? You'd said you'd be home by 10 and here it is midnight. You're a stupid, no-good kid. Get out!"

An "I-Message" alternative would be: "When you don't call me or let me know when you're coming home, I feel you may have been hurt. I was worried about you. It is important for you to call me. I know you want to be independent, but let's discuss boundaries and limits. I don't hate you. I am upset with your behavior." "I-Messages" should express how you are affected by another's behavior.

SET REALISTIC GOALS

Sometimes when we get angry at our own lack of progress, that anger is reflected or redirected at how we treat others. When we do not reach our goals, desires and hopes, frustration and feeling angry are a common consequence. Setting realistic goals for yourself will enable you to feel better and reduce any personal frustration. The net result is that you become a better person to those around you. When you see even small successes, tell yourself that you are making progress. Reassure yourself, even when you are making only small strides.

In his book, "In Praise of Plodders", Warren Wiersbe highlights four areas of stress for pastors…

Unreachable goals
Unmanageable schedules
Uncomfortable situations
Unbearable problems

AVOID "SHOULD'S"

Setting tight requirements or high expectations for yourself or others is a common problem that can lead to stress and more anger. You know when you are setting unrealistic expectations when you find yourself frequently saying that people <u>should</u> be or do something other than what they are actually capable of doing. Examples of "shoulds" are:

"She/he should be more loving."

"When I walk into, people should immediately say hello to me."

"When I assigned the job, she should have completed it right away."

"They should show me more respect. After all, I'm their superior. I deserve it."

Psalm 37:8 (NLT)
Stop being angry! Turn from your rage! Do not lose your temper—it only leads to harm.

PERFECTIONISM SCALE (PE)

YOUR RISK LEVEL _____

The Perfectionism Scale assesses the need to think and behave in perfectionistic ways toward self and others. Perfectionism is not the search for excellence – it is the search for unobtainable and unrealistic goals, standards and expectations. The net result is stress...both internally as well as externally with coworkers, family and friends.

WHAT TO KNOW

A high score on the **Perfectionism Scale** is correlated with chronic health and emotional problems and is an important stress warning sign. Individuals caught up in perfectionist thinking and behaving can experience significant personal distress accompanied by physical and emotional problems. Their unrealistically high standards and quest to avoid failure can also produce strong negative responses from others who may not share the same values or standards. If you scored high or medium on the Perfectionism Scale, recognize that your perfectionism may be damaging to your health and quality of life.

Perfectionism is not the same as making a conscientious effort to do your personal best. Seeking excellence is a realistic goal that generates a feeling of personal satisfaction. Perfectionists, however, set the bar so high that their expectations are not achievable. The result is stress due to unfulfilled expectations.

Perfectionists strive to be organized and on top of every detail. And, regardless of their level of achievement, they come away feeling they have fallen short of their goal. Perfection is illusive, and generally speaking, unattainable. The net effect is an overwhelming and continuous sense of disappointment and unhappiness.

Perfectionism is a learned behavior. It is the result of years of external (imposed by others) and internal (self-imposed) pressure to improve one's own performance. Perfectionistic thinking is based on the unrealistic belief that, "Unless I am perfect, I am not okay." Perfectionists believe they cannot be happy unless they are perfect. Over time, this can use the stress response to cause health and social problems.

GOD IS NOT LOOKING FOR PERFECTION, HE IS LOOKING FOR FAITHFULNESS.

Colossians 3:23 (NIV)
"Whatever you do, work at it with all your heart, as working for the Lord, not for human masters, since you know that you will receive an inheritance from the Lord as a reward. It is the Lord Christ you are serving.

WHAT TO DO

SET REALISTIC EXPECTATIONS

Perfectionists should re-evaluate and, when appropriate, readjust their expectations for themselves, as well as for others who do not meet their needs. Most perfectionists set extremely high standards for themselves and others. Setting high standards is not the problem. Setting standards that cannot be realistically attained can be emotionally damaging to you as well as to others whom you care about.

Evaluate expectations to determine if you are trying to do too much, for too many and in too short a time period. Also, determine if you expect too much from others, particularly those close to you. Perhaps you are holding expectations for a child, volunteer or your spouse that are unreasonable. Goals that "stretch" people are fine and desirable. Goals that "break" people create stress.

Philippians 4:6
Do not be anxious about anything, but in every situation, by prayer and petition, with thanksgiving, present your requests to God. 7 And the peace of God, which transcends all understanding, will guard your hearts and your minds in Christ Jesus.

MASTER FEAR OF FAILURE

Since fear of failure motivates the perfectionist, one should ask: "What is the worst thing that could happen if I didn't do this task perfectly. What if I am not perceived as being perfect?" Generally, the answer to these questions is not as dire as one might imagine. People will not reject you or think less of you if, in fact, things are not perfect. The imagined consequences are typically greater than reality.

Practice leaving some things undone or less "perfect" than your normal performance. Most things can wait a day or two. Distinguish between life's essentials and nonessentials, so you know where to place your time and energy. Misplaced effort results in disappointment. Some tasks need to be done very well; others can be done less perfectly or even haphazardly. Strive for excellence only when excellence is required; be perfectionistic only when perfectionism is really achievable.

Finally, failing to reach your goals is not necessarily a sign of failure and is certainly not a sign that you as a person could be labeled a "failure". Failure is relative to your ideals and values. Keeping standards reasonable does not mean you will necessarily develop an ineffective program or produce less. In fact, many people only succeed after repeated failures. For some, it contributes to their eventual success.

LET GO

Focus on the practice of "letting go." Remember, there is a time to turn off the computer, put the pen down, turn the phone off store and call it a day. When you let go, stress will flow away from you; the result is that you actually feel better and become more relaxed.

Perfectionists often do not know their needs or how to meet them. When you stop and take time for yourself, your deeper needs will begin to rise into your awareness. To fulfill those deeper needs, you must fight the mental tapes that you unconsciously say to yourself such as: "do more, be better, work harder and never stop."

Try talking to yourself in a new and more productive way. For example, use words that reassure yourself such as, "I am good enough. I can rest now. I do not need to be perfect in everything I do. I deserve to do something just for myself."

We all use self-talk to direct our behaviors and actions. Changing your self-talk and using new and more positive words will make a difference in how you feel. Make the phrase, "Let It Go", become an integral part of your thinking and stress will automatically dissipate.

WHEN YOU AIM FOR PERFECTION, YOU DISCOVER IT'S A MOVING TARGET.

TIME-URGENCY SCALE (TI)

YOUR RISK LEVEL _____

Today more people than ever are in a rush to move faster and do more in less time. While a "go-get-'em" attitude can be the spark which makes great things happen, an excessive amount of time urgency can cause personal stress. With the explosion in information technology, constant text messaging and e-mailing, living each day by the "smart" phone, the external and internal pressure we place upon ourselves to do more and to do it quicker is causing increased physical and emotional problems.

WHAT TO KNOW

Ecclesiastes 3:1 (NIV)
There is a time for everything, and a season for every activity under the heavens.

Excessive Time-Urgency is a classic component of the Type-A personality. Individuals who are overly time-oriented risk more cardiovascular, gastrointestinal and other health problems than those who work at a more relaxed and steady pace. Excessive Time-Urgency keeps the mind and body at high anxiety and stress levels.

Individuals who constantly perceive life in a time-urgent way tend to worry excessively about schedules, set overly-tight deadlines, rush when rushing is not necessary and constantly multi-task. These self-defeating behaviors and thoughts create stress and rob enjoyment from work and, even, play. The key is to develop solid time mastery skills that will enable you to "walk" not "run" through life. If you scored medium to high on this scale, slow down and take life and events as they are and not as you think they <u>should</u> be. Learn to manage your time and you will help defeat this negative thinking.

Matthew 6:25-34 (NIV)
"Therefore I tell you, do not worry about your life, what you will eat or drink; or about your body, what you will wear. Is not life more than food, and the body more than clothes? Look at the birds of the air; they do not sow or reap or store away in barns, and yet your heavenly Father feeds them. Are you not much more valuable than they? Can any one of you by worrying add a single hour to your life?

WHAT TO DO

MAKE TIME YOUR FRIEND

Time can be your enemy or your friend. When time is your friend, you take a more relaxed approach to work or play. If you make time your enemy, you see time being drained away and your anxiety increases.

Time-Urgency is a perception problem. Everyone has some time pressure to get things done, meet occasional tight deadlines, and have places to go. This behavior is now common place in our ever accelerated society. When you place everything under time pressure, stress erupts. Rethink your view of time. Ask: "Does this relationship reflect what is really important to me?" Place events, tasks and time in their proper perspective.

SLOW DOWN AND LISTEN

Practice doing some things slowly. Not all tasks need to be done quickly. Take a child's view in which tasks are done in the time it takes to do them. When you are talking with people, LISTEN more than you talk. Little is learned when we do the talking. By listening more and talking less you slow down and actually hear what the other person is saying. Under stress, we reduce our ability to interpret what a person is saying. Quiet listening reduces stress.

Prov. 17:27
The one who has knowledge uses words with restraint, and whoever has understanding is even-tempered.

SEPARATE WORK FROM PLAY

Keep work and play separate. Work does have more time requirements than play. Don't apply the requirements of work to your social gatherings. Think about it. Do you behave as though social activities are board meetings?

CHANGE YOUR EXPECTATIONS

Expecting that you must always do more and do it faster is at the root of a Time-Urgency problem. Determine if you are trying to do more than you are reasonably capable of doing. Focus on one thing at a time. Try to keep expectations of yourself and others in-line with reality. Since negative "self-talk" and improper expectations are the cause of your stress, learn to constantly check what you are expecting of yourself. Ask yourself, "Is this a reasonable and realistic expectation?" If not, change your expectation. If your expectation is realistic, then go forward with the task.

LEARN TO DEAL WITH FEAR OF REJECTION

Many people operating in the HURRY MODE fear rejection and disapproval. Trying to please everyone by rushing to meet "their" needs is the problem. If you **must** make all your appointments on time or, if you **must** never be late, you may have an excessive need to please others. Ask yourself, "If I fail to live up to someone's expectations, what's the worst that could happen?"

People often want to make their crisis yours. Avoid the temptation of making other peoples crisis yours. In most cases it took them a long time to get to this point and it won't be solved overnight.

TIMELINESS, NOT TIME-URGENCY

Being on time is necessary for most situations and meetings. However, while it is important to be on time for most appointments, not all require a "do-or-die" attitude. It really is not necessary to rush through traffic, risking life and limb, just to avoid being late. So, take the foot off the gas, take a deep breath and relax. All will be well.

BE A GOOD PLANNER

Rushing around may indicate a deeper problem such as a lack of plannig. Do you know which things are more important than others? Do you fall into the trap of "failing to plan" and then wind up rushing at the last minute to get the job done? Evaluate your planning and organizing skills to see if you can reduce the stress caused by poor planning.

Proverbs 21:5 (NIV)
The plans of the diligent lead to profit as surely as haste leads to poverty.

"The greatest weapon against stress is our ability to choose one thought over another."
William James

DISAPPOINTMENT SCALE (DI)

YOUR RISK LEVEL _____

Research has shown that those who scored high on the Disappointment (DI) Scale had a greater frequency of physical or emotional difficulties than those who scored low. Individuals who experience a high level of disappointment tend to have more headaches, gastrointestinal difficulties, moist palms, over-perspiration and other physical problems than those scoring low on this scale.

WHAT TO KNOW

Disappointment relates to what you expect from others or from life in general. Some disappointment is unavoidable, while at other times it is preventable or, at least, somewhat avoidable. Disappointment that is unavoidable includes events such as decrease in business revenues, laying off staff, family members who do not live up to your expectations or friends who move or are forced to relocate. Very little can be done to prevent these stressors from occurring.

Disappointment is a result of thinking negatively of others because they do not meet your expectations. High scorers on this scale have difficulty in setting realistic expectations for themselves or others and typically resist changing their expectations to be more in-line with reality. Their attitude is: "This is what I expect and nothing else will do."

Even if you think your expectations are appropriate and realistic, they may not be. For example, you call a friend several times and she does not reciprocate. You're upset, angry and disappointed. You "write her off" as a friend. However, the reality may be quite different. She may want to call but is overworked, out-of-town or simply overwhelmed with her personal life. Perhaps she is not time oriented and forgets and fails to do what she knows she should do, not because she doesn't like you, but because of her nature. You either accept her as is, or adjust to make the relationship work if it's important to you.

All of us experience disappointment to some extent; however, some of us are more prone to feeling disappointed when our expectations are not met by the people around us. Feeling repeatedly disappointed is a result of a pattern of faulty or irrational thinking about the person or situation. If you experience frequent disappointment, evaluate your expectations and, if necessary, you may need to alter or lower them to be more in-line with what is actually possible.

WHAT TO DO

WHAT'S REAL AND WHAT ISN'T

If you learn to differentiate between avoidable and unavoidable stressors, you will have greater control over how you respond and, consequently, you will be able to reduce personal discouragement and disappointment. Focus on changing an event that is, indeed, changeable. One way to reduce your disappointment is to create realistic expectations from the beginning. Realize that faulty thinking may be at the heart of your excessive disappointment and work to understand that <u>what you think affects how you feel.</u>

CHANGE EXPECTATIONS

Expectations play the central role in disappointment and the resulting stress. Evaluate what you expect from family, friends, church members and volunteers. What do you expect from life, God, spouse, coworkers or your children? Mentally check to see if your expectations are reasonable and achievable. If not, you may need to change or alter your expectations. However, if your expectations are reasonable, then go with them.

Determine if your disappointment is specific to one person or situation or to most aspects of your life. This will allow you to focus your energies more effectively. Write down specific disappointments or examples of disappointment and look for the cause, not just the symptom of your stress.

Ask someone close to you if they think your expectations are out-of-line with what is reasonable. They may have a better, or at least a different, perspective than you. Listen to what they say. "If the shoe fits," it is up to you to make the necessary change. Remember, the only control you have is the control you place on your own thinking, not the attitudes and behaviors of others. We can influence, ask, request, even demand, but ultimately, you control only YOU and no one else.

REDIRECT YOUR THINKING

Romans 12:2
Do not conform to the pattern of this world, but be transformed by the renewing of your mind. Then you will be able to test and approve what God's will is—his good, pleasing and perfect will.

Your thinking determines your expectations. The good news is that thinking is controllable. Keep in mind that while you have some control over your thoughts, you have no control over the thoughts or action of others.

Direct your thoughts away from the concern you have with the people who are not meeting your hopes and desires. If someone consistently cannot or will not give you what you want, you have choices; i.e., accept the person as he or she or choose to limit your time with them or dependency on them. Make this kind of decision with care.

STOP DWELLING!

Dwelling on a disappointment is "mental obsession." It doesn't change a person or what they may have done to you. Being preoccupied with a person who does not meet your needs creates unnecessary stress. When you catch yourself thinking excessively about a recent disappointment, redirect and focus back on letting go and accepting that person for who they are. Being in "the moment" is the key to nurturing a positive view of the situation and that will help you feel better. The first step to thinking clearly is to lower your stress levels. Anxiety and fear interferes with rational thinking. Do some deep breathing, take a slow relaxed walk, sit back and focus on the moment...then begin to redirect your thoughts.

COMMUNICATE MORE EFFECTIVELY

When you think about it, you have little or no control over the actions of others. You can, however, have some influence over people through good and clear communication. You will have better success in getting people to change or do what you desire by employing better communication and effective listening techniques.

James 1:19 (NIV)
"My dear brothers and sisters, take note of this: Everyone should be quick to listen, slow to speak and slow to become angry."

BECOME A BETTER LISTENER

Listen actively and listen more to what others are really trying to communicate. By understanding the person, your expectations become more realistic and achievable. You will also feel much better. Plus, you may see some changes in his or her behavior and attitude.

One of the most effective communication tools involves stating what you want from someone and then asking that person to restate what you said. Simply asking for the person to restate what you said will insure that your message got through. They may choose to ignore or not do what you ask, but at least they know exactly what they want and expect.

In turn, you can use the same technique when someone expresses their desires and expectations for you. Start with: "If I understand you correctly, what you are saying is..." This is a simple, but powerful, tool. Ultimately, you can reduce or eliminate disappointment through better clarification of what is being said or heard.

Stress Resilient people check their expectations to see if they are in-line with what is achievable. If what is expected is really not possible, they readjust their thinking to accurately reflect reality.

BURNOUT SCALE (BR)

YOUR RISK LEVEL _____

Frequent periods of negative moods are a clear stress warning sign. Individuals who scored high on the Burnout (BR) Scale are likely to be experiencing greater stress than those who scored low. If you scored medium to high on this scale, evaluate what you are thinking and what is the source of your feelings. Is your thinking positive or negative? Do you frequently think about the worst of situations, people or yourself? Are your thoughts mostly negative and do you feel down? The key to feeling better is to make changes in how you view yourself and the world around you. Keep in mind that Burnout is not the same as depression or, even, manic-depression. These are clinical conditions that require competent professional attention from a psychologist or mental health professional.

WHAT TO KNOW

There are a number of things that church leaders can do to avoid burnout but first and foremost remember, you are not God, He can get along and get things done without you, and for whatever reason only He knows, he chooses to use you out of grace. You are not the Savior to the church, nor are you to do the work of the Spirit within the church, you and others, are the tools He uses to do the work of the ministry within the church.

People whose life is filled with both major life changes and a large amount of daily hassles often become "burned-out" and discouraged. Some burnout is normal. Most of us experience it. When burnout occurs frequently or with intensity, focus on finding ways to reverse the negative thinking which generates and maintains these moods.

Philippians 4:8 (NLT)
"And now, dear brothers and sisters, one final thing. Fix your thoughts on what is true, and honorable, and right, and pure, and lovely, and admirable. Think about things that are excellent and worthy of praise."

Periods of negative mood or feeling "burned-out" may be an indication that stress is having an effect on your body and quality of your life. Recent research has shown that individuals experiencing burnout experience changes in the frequency and amount of stress hormones, such as cortisol, in their bodies. These hormones can produce the feeling of being down and "lifeless". The more you feel this way, the greater the stress.

As with most stress "coping" mechanisms, burnout is the result of prolonged periods of hassles and major life events that lead to increasingly negative thoughts and perceptions about oneself and the world in general.

Frequent occurrences of negative mood indicate that stress is affecting you detrimentally. You may be experiencing personal burnout. You may also be trying to communicate with others in an indirect way that you are unhappy with yourself, them or life in general. Showing the world how bad you feel may be a plea for help. Unfortunately, those around you may not be able to interpret your moods, nor know what to do.

Some negative mood may not be avoidable. Occasional "down" times may have a cleansing effect; e.g., after being rejected for a new position, you feel hurt and "blue". This is a normal reaction to your "perceived" failure. As you work through those moments, you will realize that there are things you can do to improve the situation such as: move, apply for another position, or simply talk to your leadership about what you can do to improve yourself. Your mood lifts and you feel more in control.

Burnout is often the result of irrational thinking. A common irrational thought is to <u>focus on the negative and not see the positive in life.</u> For example, your spouse does not tell you he loves you. You interpret this as "he doesn't love me anymore". You may discover that with some rational thinking you too have stopped saying, "I love you"– not because you don't love him, but because perhaps you've been too preoccupied and worn-out from work. You realize that love is there, but you and your spouse are just not saying what's in your hearts.

One cause of negative mood is the self-talk called <u>stinkin' thinkin'</u>. Ironically, because you are not changing the thoughts or attitudes that cause negative feelings to occur, the more you focus on trying to change how bad you feel, the less those feelings change.

WHAT TO DO

KNOW WHERE FEELINGS COME FROM

Feelings usually follow, not precede, your thinking. It is mostly through our thoughts and mental images that produce feelings like anxiety, sadness and anger. It is a fallacy that you must first feel good <u>before</u> you can do something. There are many things you can do. For example, imagine a very positive time in your life when you felt great. If you really picture it, you will feel some of the warm and good feelings of that time. Focus your thoughts and visualizations on good experiences and your feelings will begin to change. It is a fact: "Negative thinking produces negative feelings. And, positive thinking produces positive feelings."

Joshua 1:8 (NIV)
"Keep this Book of the Law always on your lips; meditate on it day and night, so that you may be careful to do everything written in it. Then you will be prosperous and successful."

Ultimately, you have more control over your feelings than you may realize. It takes work, but even little changes in your self-talk can make an immediate difference in how you feel. You can change your mood without the of use drugs or medications. But, to do so will require focusing on changing any faulty, negative or distorted thinking patterns.

There are exceptions. Feelings can come from physiological imbalances from too much alcohol or other drugs. Hormonal changes and imbalances can also be a factor…even for men. Major depression may be the result of inherited neurological imbalances. If a feeling has a physiological basis, changing thinking will help, but may not be able to override the chemical basis for the problem. Check to see if depression is caused by medical problems.

Isaiah 40:28
Do you not know? Have you not heard? The Lord is the everlasting God, the Creator of the ends of the earth. He will not grow tired or weary, and his understanding no one can fathom. 29 He gives strength to the weary and increases the power of the weak. 30 Even youths grow tired and weary, and young men stumble and fall; 31 but those who hope in the Lord will renew their strength. They will soar on wings like eagles; they will run and not grow weary, they will walk and not be faint.

IS IT REAL DEPRESSION?

Depression and negative moods are closely linked but are not the same. If you think you are <u>chronically depressed</u>, have no energy or desire to make changes in your life and not just experiencing the normal ups and downs of everyday living, seek professional help–immediately. If you have a work Employee Assistance Program (EAP), call them today. If not, seek out professional assistance from a psychologist or mental health professional.

CHANGE IRRATIONAL THOUGHTS

Irrational thinking is at the heart of feeling down or blue. For example, you may think you are a failure, but you may actually be a success. You choose not to see the good in you. You may think, "I never do anything right". Or, "No one could love someone like me". Do a reality check. Ask: "Are my assumptions correct?" If not, it may be time to change what you are thinking.

Definition: Assume – The lowest form of knowledge. When you make decisions or plan responses based on assumptions you are using the lowest form of knowledge at your disposal. The reality is, you don't know. So avoid reactions based on assumptions until you have evidence to do so.

There are many types of irrational thoughts, here are a few of the more common irrational thoughts:

- ***EXTREMIST THINKING***

You view everything as all bad or all good. Most situations are a mix of good and bad. Someone makes a mistake and you think the world has come to an end.

- ***STOMPING ON THE POSITIVE***

You choose not to see the good in a situation. Like a wet blanket on a fire, you stomp on anything positive. A positive comment is made about someone you do not like and you "jump" all over the person.

- ***DWELLING ON THE NEGATIVE***

You filter in only the negative aspects of life. By becoming obsessed with the negative, you make yourself a slave to your thinking. You may be obsessed with mostly the bad experiences in your life and not the good.

- ***ESP THINKING***

You think you know how others feel and think about you, or, even worse, you expect others to know what you think or feel. (Review the definition of "Assume")

- ***OVER GENERALIZING***

A few bad things happen. Consequently, you think everything is going to fall apart. Recognize the error of overgeneralization and tell yourself that everything will not fall apart just because a few bad or difficult things have happened. Success usually follows failure.

Changing self-talk is a challenge because we've programmed ourselves to think about people and life in a particular way. This is the "internal chatter" that can bring us down. But, when you cannot change what you think, change your behavior; do something new or different. The solution resides in action. Take a walk, ride a bike, visit a friend, read a book. Seek professional help if nothing seems to work.

UNDERACHIEVEMENT SCALE (UA)

YOUR RISK LEVEL _____

High scorers on the Underachievement (UA) Scale believe that they are living unproductive or unsuccessful lives. Underachievers think this way even when there is objective proof that they are in fact achieving much in their lives. People who feel they are unproductive tend to feel dissatisfied, which, in turn, can produce a variety of physical and emotional problems. Ironically, both the quality and quantity of their work, not to mention other areas of their lives, can be negatively affected.

If you scored high on the Underachievement Scale, learn more about how to mobilize yourself in positive and productive directions. (See "What To Do" in the Time Urgency section).

Like all stress indicators, the perception of underachievement may be the result of faulty self-perceptions. Ironically, even a highly productive person can perceive themselves as underachieving. Learning to have a rational view of your life and personal productivity will help you conquer the perception of underachievement.

WHAT TO KNOW

The perception of underachievement is at the core of self-disappointment. While excessive disappointment is largely related to disappointment with other people, underachievement is related to disappointment with ourselves and what we view as our shortcomings and mistakes.

Underachievers perceive they are failing to accomplish what they set out to do with their lives. They feel frustrated that they are not accomplishing what they had expected or, they may feel, they are not achieving their goals fast enough. For example, a highly "successful" insurance person, who reached all her goals and was the most successful person in her agency, perceived that she was an underachiever. This happened because she had set herself up for failure with goals and expectations that were not realistic. Her expectations for herself were extremely unrealistic and too high. Changing them made a difference in her stress levels and how she felt about herself.

The perception of any underachievement is directly related to your perception of what you think you can and should be achieving. Any negative self-talk as to why you are not achieving what you want from yourself should be changed to become more positive and self-reassuring.

WHAT TO DO

Philippians 4:12 (NIV),
"I know what it is to be in need, and I know what it is to have plenty. I have learned the secret of being content in any and every situation, whether well fed or hungry, whether living in plenty or in want."

Many of the concepts and ideas expressed in the Disappointment Scale section apply to those who are chronically feeling that they are underachieving. These concepts are not repeated here. (Review "What to Know" and "What To Do" in the Disappointment Scale section).

FACT OR FANTASY?

The view that one is underachieving is directly related to the goals and expectations set and the degree to which one is meeting those expectations. If you set unrealistic goals for yourself, such as I'll be a millionaire by 30, then you will most likely feel like an underachiever.

There are several things you can do to insure that you do not feel like an underachiever or failure. First, determine if there is a sound and rational basis for your underachievement. You may be correct that you have the capability and skill to achieve more. You may have a patent or invention that will indeed make millions for you. But, if you do not have an immediate way to reach your goal, then consider lowering or moderating your expectations to a more realistic time frame.

Second, take stock of what you are doing with your life at home and work and look for those things that you are actually accomplishing. You may be disregarding positive achievements and only looking at the negative.

At home, for example, you have a very loving family and you are always there for your children or spouse. At work, recognize what you have done for your church or yourself over the past year and acknowledge that you are in fact doing many things very well.

Third, take a broader look at life and don't over generalize when things don't go as expected. If you only occasionally fail to meet your own expectations, then look more closely at other areas of your life to reassure yourself.

Last, if you frequently fail to meet your expectations, ask yourself, "Did I really miss the mark? Did I truly fail at what I set out to do?" Take a different perspective. Perhaps there are other ways to measure success. Avoid thinking of success as all or nothing. Consider that satisfaction in life comes from a quest for constant improvement and not the actual achievement of a single goal.

CHANGE PERSPECTIVES

Romans 8:28
And we know that God causes everything to work together for the good of those who love God and are called according to his purpose for them.

Achieving a goal is good, but you will always look back at the process of reaching that goal as the most satisfying part—the quest! People fail every day. Most people come very close to succeeding and miss the "mark" by only a little. Only underachievers interpret this as failure.

Evaluate your situation very carefully. If your underachievement is a fallacy and you really are accomplishing much, ask yourself, "Am I setting myself up for failure by not evaluating my goals correctly?" If unrealistic expectations result in the perception of underachievement, scale down or modify what you expect. Work to develop more realistic expectations in future situations. Setting unrealistically high expectations for yourself guarantees you will feel disappointed. Such thinking often lowers self-esteem and increases stress.

DEVELOP NEW SKILLS

If you are not accomplishing what you want in life, both at home and work, evaluate your skills to see if you need more training or skill building. Many people fail because they lack the necessary skills to foster success. Always keep on learning.

BEGIN WITH THE END IN MIND

Stephen Covey, in his book the 7 Habits of Highly Effective People (see Resources at the end of this booklet) points out to Begin With The End in Mind as his first principle. Not reaching our goals is often a result of a lack of a clear view of what you want to accomplish.

BECOME A BETTER PLANNER

Once you have a clear goal in mind, remember that underachievement often results from poor planning, inadequate organization, and other "controllable" factors. Learn how to take action to improve your skills and behavior in these critical areas. Seek assistance from those who know how to plan, organize and follow through with plans. Attend workshops and seminars, read books or listen to tapes on being more productive and organized. Learn better time management skills. Better organize yourself, your office, or your home.

BECOME MORE POSITIVE

Mild or severe depression can also cause one to underachieve. If you are depressed and this is indeed affecting your life and work, seek professional help. Review the section on Burnout. Ultimately, to feel better you will need to change your thinking about some aspects of your life.

TENSION SCALE (TE)

YOUR RISK LEVEL _____

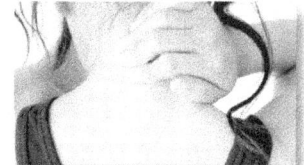

A high score on the Tension Scale (TE) indicates a high level of physical and emotional tension in your body. Those who score high on this scale rarely take time to relax and release inner tension. As a result, highly tense people do not enjoy good physical and emotional health. If you scored medium to high on this scale, you probably have more stress and discomfort than others who score low. Begin to create more time to relax and you will counteract the negative effect of stress.

Under prolonged tension, the body begins to produce a change in all of your body systems including: muscles, endocrine, digestive, cardiovascular and other bodily systems. One common complaint from too much tension and stress is pain. Pain is often the result of prolonged tension in one or more areas of the body. For example, headaches are very common these days and are usually the result of muscles being unknowingly constricted for hours.

WHAT TO KNOW

Many physical problems are associated with chronic tension; one is chronic fatigue. Chronic fatigue is produced from both the physical and mental tension within us. Some people are so fatigued that they can barely work. Yet, they push on…only to make matters worse.

Not taking time to "relax" is an important indicator of stress. Some people think that just relaxing in front of a TV set is the way to go. While this form of relaxation is OK, it does not accomplish the goal of bringing down body tension.

Deep relaxation is the process of allowing the body to let go and reduce inner physical and emotional tension; it is a conscious act of mentally "letting go" accompanied by intentionally focusing on something positive that lifts our spirit and builds our faith. Ask yourself, "What is the value you place on taking time for yourself?" This will determine if you will become a relaxed person in a tense world.

Very tense individuals experience the consequences of prolonged stress in muscle tension, physical pain and fatigue. These individuals tend to also have a higher than normal rate of errors and mistakes at work or in their daily lives. When the body is tense, one does not see, hear or, even, process ideas very well. Consequently, more errors are produced than would normally be expected.

For example, employees who work for long hours at a computer without interruption experience increase muscle tension and fatigue. Many workers who do repetitive work develop a host of physical aches and pains that can result in errors, mistakes and, ultimately, lower productivity. However, those individuals who take time to bring down tension through periodic breaks, deep relaxation exercises and meditation function better and become more productive.

On the emotional side, overly tense people often feel incredibly guilty about taking it easy and being good to themselves and their bodies. They rarely take lunch breaks, read books, or take walks. When they do, they feel guilty. The core cause of this behavior is a value system which says, "The only thing good…is to work! Play and relaxation is sinful". This error in thinking does little to foster good stress resilience or STRESSMASTERY.

In general, not taking time to relax can results in:

Mental burnout
Increased errors
Poor decision making
Head, neck & back pain
Reduced physical energy
Reduced quality of work
Difficulty concentrating
Avoidance of others

WHAT TO DO

TAKE TIME FOR YOU

Mark 6:46 (NLT)
"After telling everyone good-bye,
he went up into the hills by himself to pray."

Are you giving too much to others and not enough for yourself? Do you want to take time for yourself, but just can't seem to make it happen? Do you really believe that if you stop work to relax for 10-15 minutes, the job will never get done? Many people believe that taking time to do relaxation exercises, for example, is a waste of time. Not so. Research shows that taking relaxation breaks actually improves performance.

guilty about it. JUST DO IT! When people feel guilty about taking time for themselves and doing something they enjoy, they often stop doing it. Then, resentment sets in and the potential benefits are lost. Don't live your life through other people's standards and expectations. Set you own standard and change the mental tape that says "It's wrong to take care of yourself or it's a sin to focus on yourself."

Take control of your guilt-producing thoughts and tell yourself that "it is okay and good for you to take time for yourself and enjoy life." Focus on the benefits to you and your family that will occur when you are more relaxed and energized.

GO TO LUNCH AND DON'T RUSH

Take a long and relaxed lunch break several times a week. Don't do business. Take a friend with you and enjoy good conversation. Volunteer your time for a good cause. Read a novel over a cup of tea. Go to a museum. Sit quietly by a stream, in a park or in your own car where no one can reach you. By the way, eat slowly.

WALK EVERY DAY!

Walk by yourself or with a friend. Talk not about problems, but possibilities. Walking 30 minutes a day will reduce stress and tension and improve your health! When you walk, look around you and notice the world before you. Look at the trees, flowers, people and children and, yes, stop and smell the roses.

Mark 6:31
Then Jesus said,
"Let's go off by ourselves to a quiet place and rest awhile." He said this because there were so many people coming and going that Jesus and his apostles didn't even have time to eat.

EXERCISE MORE

Exercise is the number one way to bring down tension and reduce stress. It takes up to 24 hours for the body to purge stress hormones, but with exercise those hormones are gone in just 2 hours.

Join an aerobics class, go to the gym, play tennis, ride a bike, hike on weekends, go to a fitness center or jog with friends. You will feel better.

LEARN TO MEDITATE!

*Psalm 145:5 (NLT),
I will meditate on your majestic,
glorious splendor and your wonderful miracles.*

Biblical Meditation is about focus. As we ponder and reflect on Christ, we are better able to internalize His precepts in a deeper, more transforming way. Meditation is not simply focusing on our feelings, intuition, exercise, detachment or manipulation, to get what we want from God or a deeper sense of ourselves. Biblical meditation has its foundation in the Lord, who equips us to meet the emotional, physical, and spiritual needs of one another. It is drawing our attention to Christ-to whom He is and what He has done for us.

DECOMPRESS.

Scuba divers who spend long periods of time at significant depths have to incorporate decompression stops into their dive times before returning to the surface. This is due to the stress placed on their bodies from the pressure of the water. The pressure of the atmosphere on our bodies at the surface (14.7 psi) increases by one atmosphere of pressure for every 30 feet you go below the surface. Because divers breath compressed air, nitrogen builds up in the body and if ascending too quickly would cause it to be forced out of the body rapidly resulting in bubbles in the blood stream, which can be fatal.

On their ascent they may have additional oxygen tanks attached to their ascension line in order to spend the amount of time required at each decompression point for the nitrogen to slowly dissipate. This process allows their body to adjust to the decreasing pressure providing a safe ascent.

In a similar manner we can apply this to the stress of leadership. Build decompression stops into your schedule, between meetings or appointments, after prolonged periods of increased pressure, which may require longer periods of rest time. Don't try to live with the increased pressure of stress for long periods of time and not build decompression stops into your schedule.

LISTEN TO RELAXATION TAPES

Audio relaxation tapes are an excellent way to learn how to let go and relax. To develop the skill of deep relaxation takes time and, yes, dedication. But, the end result will be less stress and the body will cleanse itself of damaging stress hormones and chemicals.

LISTEN TO RELAXING MUSIC

Music is an excellent way to reduce stress. Many forms of music can help you to let go and relax. Everyone has a music preference. Generally you want to listen to music that is soothing and calm. Some classical or contemporary music are particularly helpful for reducing stress.

STRESSMASTER INTERNATIONAL
STRESS EFFECTS SCALES

The result of prolonged stress can be chronic physical and emotional dis-stress. Since the effects of stress are the main indicators of how well you are mastering stress, these are important concepts for to understand. If you scored high on either or both of these scales, it will be important to learn new and better ways to bring down your stress levels each day. Keep in mind that these scales provide an insight to the degree that stress <u>may</u> be affecting you.

How did you do on the SMQ? Place a (X) in the space below that corresponds to your score on the following SMQ Scales.

The 2 scales that make up the **Stress Effects Scales** are:

	Low	Medium-Low	Medium	Medium-High	High
Physical Effects (PE)	_____	_____	_____	_____	_____
LIfe/Work Satisfaction (L/W)	_____	_____	_____	_____	_____

Comments/Notes: How is stress affecting you?

PHYSICAL STRESS EFFECTS SCALE (PE)

YOUR RISK LEVEL _____

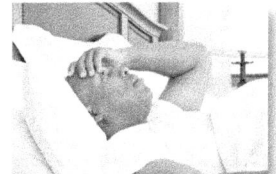

The Physical Stress Effects Scale assesses the possible affect of intense or prolonged stress on the body. Research has shown that individuals scoring medium to high on one or more of the Seven Stress Warning Signs Scales (see previous section) also have a tendency to score high on the this scale. The PE Scale is like a compass that points to how stress may be having a detrimental effect on you. For people who score high, look to see if stress may be having an impact on your current health or emotional condition. If you are in distress, it is important to see a physician or mental health professional. Seek help if you have any questions or concerns about your health, physical problems or symptoms if they are of concern to you.

If you scored medium to high on this scale or if you feel that you are experiencing frequent headaches, stomach problems, or neck and back pains, begin the process of developing the STRESSMASTERY skills suggested under the previous section called Seven Stress Warning Signs.

If you scored low on this scale, you are doing great. However, if at any time you begin to see an increase in physical problems consider that stress may be playing a role in those problems. Perhaps you are experiencing more stressors than usual (See the following Section). An increase in stressors, both major Life Events as well as Hassles, may be a time to be on guard.

LIFE/WORK SATISFACTION (LW)

YOUR RISK LEVEL _____

The LW Scale assesses emotional satisfaction with different aspects of your work and personal life. As with the PE Scale, this scale offers a glimpse of the consequences of stress on feelings and emotions and measures the level of happiness with key aspects of your life.

High levels of dissatisfaction in one area can result in unhappiness in other areas. A person who is dissatisfied with his or her career choice can easily bring that dissatisfaction into their home life. When one is dissatisfied, they may show it through anger or, possibly depression. Likewise, a person experiencing dissatisfaction and unhappiness with their family life can see an impact on their quality or quantity of work. In addition, their relationship with coworkers can also be negatively affected.

WHAT TO KNOW

The Life/Work Satisfaction Scale measures the effect of stress on personal job/work happiness. This scale can guide you toward those areas where a personal change can improve the quality of your life at work or at home. Only you can make the changes. If you scored medium to high on this scale, you are clearly dissatisfied with one or more areas of your life. This is a stress warning sign. If you have been experiencing high levels of dissatisfaction for some time, take a closer look at the causes of your dissatisfaction. Pay special attention to the Disappointment, Burnout, and Underachievement Scales of the Seven Stress Warning Signs.

WHAT TO DO

Understand that the Stress Response is both a "friend" and "foe". The impact of the Stress Response can help you to be creative and productive or, if it continues unabated, it can effect you physically and emotionally.

Since these two scales are reflection of stress, the key to reducing the negative impact is to learn the Relaxation Response. Also, review the "WHAT TO DO" sections of each Seven Stress Warning Signs areas for the knowledge and skills that will increase your STRESSMASTERY abilities. Learning how to reduce tension, stress and anxiety is ultimately up to you.

The Stress Response

So, you're under stress. What happens to your body? The Stress Response, or Fight or Flight Response, is a well researched and medically accepted concept. Yet, while the neurochemistry of the stress response is clearly known, what is not known is exactly how the various hormones affect one another and interact on the body's various organs and systems. What we do know is that these hormones play an important part in our lives.

In response to a perceived stressor, the stress response is energized and engaged. Neurons in the hypothalamus portion of the brain trigger a secretion of two key hormones (corticotrophin and arginine-vasopressin) which then affect a neuroendocrine response producing epinephrine. Epinephrine creates a "global warning system" that turns on the production of ACTH (adrenocorticotropic hormones) from the pituitary gland. ACTH charges up the adrenal cortex where cortisol and other glucocorticoids are then dumped into the blood stream. These hormones are part of the "flight or fight" response that affects all systems of the body including: cardiovascular, respiratory, gastrointestinal, renal and endocrine changes.

The Stress Response, once engaged, can now be observed and, indirectly, experienced by others. The SMQ is one way to view how stress is affecting not only your body but, also, your daily behavior, attitudes and thoughts.

THE RELAXATION RESPONSE

The Relaxation Response is a quick and easy way to counteract the Stress Response, or as it is commonly known, the "fight or flight" response. Dr. Herbert Benson coined the term Relaxation Response as a way to combat the Fight or Flight Response.

To engage the Relaxation Response

Step 1. Sit quietly, feet on the floor and hands and shoulders relaxed. Turn off phone and shut the door. Take several deep breaths filling the upper and lower cavity of the lungs. This brings more oxygen to the brain.

Step 2. With eyes closed or open, breathe through your nose and hold your breath for 5 to 10 seconds. Let out the air from your lungs slowly through your mouth. Imaging exhaling through a straw. Be aware of your breath and continue slow, deep breathing for 10 to 20 minutes.

Sept 3. Keep your mind as passive as possible and when thoughts intrude, accept them and then turn your attention back to your breathing.

Step 4. Practice several times a day and you will learn to "engage" the Relaxation Response whenever needed.

STRESSMASTER INTERNATIONAL
STRESSORS

How did you do in this area? Place a (X) in the space below that corresponds to your score on the SMQ for both the Life Events and Hassles Scales.

Stressors are events such as earthquakes, death of a loved one, economic problems or people like an angry boss, a mean motorist, or a depressed spouse, friend or loved one. When you perceive events like these to be a threat they are called stressors. In essence, we allow stressors to throw us of balance with the result being....dis-stress.

The SMQ Stressor Scales evaluate two different types of stressors that can have an impact on how well you feel and function. Learning the difference between these two concepts can make a difference in how well you master stress.

The two **Stressor** scales are:

	Low	Medium-Low	Medium	Medium-High	High
Live Events (LE)	_____	_____	_____	_____	_____
Hassles (HA)	_____	_____	_____	_____	_____

Comments/Notes: What are your key stressors?

LIFE EVENTS (LE)

YOUR RISK LEVEL _____

The Life Events scale measure some of the more common major life events as well as daily hassles that can cause the stress response within us. The two types of stressors assessed by the SMQ, Life Events and Hassles, can also be divided into those stressors that are **unavoidable** and those that can, to some extent, be **changed** or **modified.**

If you scored high or medium-high on either the Life Events or the Hassles Scale, chances are you are experiencing a higher than normal amount of stressors in your life at this time. If you scored Medium to low, you probably are not experiencing much distress at this time. However, some life events alone can be so important that it will cause a considerable amount of stress. An example of a major life stressor that could have an overriding impact is the death of a loved one or major loss of financial stability. In these cases, you may score low on both scales, but the fact that they are so important and powerful a stressor might lead to high stress levels. Regardless of your score, evaluate each stressor to determine the best course of action.

WHAT TO KNOW

Stressors are life events that happen to us, such as having a major illness, experiencing the death of a loved one, having financial problems or dealing with people such as an angry boss, road rage motorist, or a depressed spouse, friend or loved one. When you perceive events like these to be a threat they are called stressors. In essence, we allow stressors to throw us off balance with the result being....Dis-stress. The Stressor Scales assess two different types of stressors that can have an impact on how well you feel and function. Learning the difference between these two concepts can make a difference in how well you master stress.

When you perceive a stressor, whether real or imagined, first determine if the stressor can be changed, stopped or modified. If so, then you may have some influence over the repeat or re-occurrence of that stressors. The majority of Life Events, once they happen, are not changeable.

In general the Life Events Scale is an indicator of the amount of <u>unavoidable</u> life stressors that you have experienced during the past 12 months. In addition to the total number of different Life Event stressors experienced, it is important to keep in mind that some major life events can have a stronger or more lasting impact on you than other stressors.

Each person perceives and responds to major Life Events in their own unique way. Experiencing a many major Life Events has been shown to be correlated with "future" physical problems. Due to the uniqueness of each of us and our level of ability to master stressors, it is not always predictable how a person will respond to these stressors. Sometimes there is an immediate physiological reaction, like getting the common cold, headache, or stomach problems. At other times, there is a delay between the onset of multiple negative Life Events and the development of physical problems. The degree to which major life events can affect us is related to our own ability to master stress on a daily basis.

The evidence is clear that there is a "risk" for physical problems to develop after experiencing a variety of major Life Events during the preceding year. Some examples of major Life Events stressors are...

Death of a spouse or loved one
Divorce or separation
Personal injury
Marriage or Retirement
Financial loss
Change of job status
Legal problems

WHAT TO DO

Few of these stressors are preventable and most cannot be changed, although some, such as financial loss, can be prevented by improving how you handle money such as saving more or finding ways to increase your income. Once they have occurred, there is no way to change or alter them.

ACCEPTANCE

The key to dealing with unavoidable and uncontrollable stressors is to learn to "let go" and accept the reality of the situation. This is easier said than done; yet, as emotions subside, one can gradually move from rejecting and denying the event to the inevitable acceptance.

RE-FRAME

Sometimes major life events need to be Re-Framed or put into a different context so as give it a new of more effective perspective. For example, the death of a loved one or a major illness, can be viewed from multiple perspectives. One person might say, "Why me.

What have I done to deserve this? I should have done something to have prevented this." A Re-Framing would mean thinking differently such as, "I am not in control of this situation and there is nothing I can do to change it. I will be strong and positive to help my family and friends weather this storm."

EMBRACE THE CHALLENGE

People who look at a major life stressor not as a problem but as a Challenge, do much better emotionally, physically and spiritually. These hardy personalities are the ones who tend to hold up much better. So, mentally challenge yourself to overcome the current difficulties.

Romans 8:35 & 37
Can anything ever separate us from Christ's love? Does it mean he no longer loves us if we have trouble or calamity, or are persecuted, or hungry, or destitute, or in danger, or threatened with death?.... 37 No, despite all these things, overwhelming victory is ours through Christ, who loved us.

The Stress Response is a Choice!
So, too, is the Relaxation Response!
Choose Relaxation over Tension!

HASSLES (HA) SCALE

YOUR RISK LEVEL _____

The **Hassles Scale** identifies some of the more common types of daily events that may at first glance seem minor. Hassles are those that people experience each and every day. While there are many more hassles than assessed by this scale, these are some of the key stressors you are likely to experience. You can add other types of stressors more pertinent to your job or life as needed.

WHAT TO KNOW

Job 5:7 (NIV)
"Yet man is born to trouble
as surely as sparks fly upward."

Research has shown that <u>hassles</u> may be more important in producing a strong stress response than even major Life Events. Hassles, unlike Life Events, tend to be more frequent and can be extremely irritating if experienced on a perpetual basis.

Hassles are those often little but highly irritating events or situations that cause dissatisfaction, frustration and stress. The more irritating <u>you perceive these hassles to be</u>, the greater the impact on you. Frequent and enduring hassles in our daily lives can definitely affect your emotional and physical health. Hassles range from car breakdowns and home repairs to people being late to meet you or having the boss pile on more work.

WHAT TO DO

THE RELAXATION RESPONSE IS A CHOICE

How you react to a stressor, whether that stressor is big or small, frequent or infrequent is up to you. You can choose to react with anger, frustration and irritability or you can choose to accept the stressor for what it is...just an event in your life that will eventually pass.

You can choose to take a deep breath and let stress go, or you can hang on to the problem and make it worse. Mastering stress is about Letting Go and allowing the body to come back into balance. In medicine this is call Homeostasis. To the average person this means coming back into balance.

Luke 12:27
Do Not Worry "If then you cannot do even a very little thing, why do you worry about other matters? "Consider the lilies, how they grow: they neither toil nor spin; but I tell you, not even Solomon in all his glory clothed himself like one of these. "But if God so clothes the grass in the field, which is alive today and tomorrow is thrown into the furnace, how much more will He clothe you? You men of little faith!

CHOICES: ATTITUDE IS EVERYTHING

John is the kind of guy you love to hate. He is always in a good mood and always has something positive to say. When someone would ask him how he was doing, he would reply, 'If I were any better, I would be twins!'

He was a natural motivator.

If an employee was having a bad day, John was there telling the employee how to look on the positive side of the situation.

Seeing this style really made me curious, so one day I went up and asked him, 'I don't get it!

You can't be a positive person all of the time How do you do it?'

He replied, 'Each morning I wake up and say to myself, you have two choices today. You can choose to be in a good mood or ... you can choose to be in a bad mood

I choose to be in a good mood.'

Each time something bad happens, I can choose to be a victim or...I can choose to learn from it. I choose to learn from it.

Every time someone comes to me complaining, I can choose to accept their complaining or... I can point out the positive side of life. I choose the positive side of life.

'Yeah, right, it's not that easy,' I protested.

'Yes, it is,' he said. 'Life is all about choices. When you cut away all the junk, every situation is a choice. You choose how you react to situations. You choose how people affect your mood.

You choose to be in a good mood or bad mood. The bottom line: It's your choice how you live your life.'

I reflected on what he said. Soon thereafter, I left the Tower Industry to start my own business. We lost touch, but I often thought about him when I made a choice about life instead of reacting to it.

Several years later, I heard that he was involved in a serious accident, falling some 60 feet from a communications tower.

After 18 hours of surgery and weeks of intensive care,
he was released from the hospital with rods placed in his back.

I saw him about six months after the accident.

When I asked him how he was, he replied, 'If I were any better, I'd be twins.
Wanna see my scars?'

I declined to see his wounds, but I did ask him what had gone through his mind
as the accident took place.

'The first thing that went through my mind was the well-being of my soon-to-be born daughter,'
he replied. 'Then, as I lay on the ground, I remembered that I had two choices: I could choose to
live or...I could choose to die. I chose to live.'

'Weren't you scared? Did you lose consciousness?' I asked

He continued, '...the paramedics were great.

They kept telling me I was going to be fine. But when they wheeled me into the ER and I saw the
expressions on the faces of the doctors and nurses, I got really scared.. In their eyes, I read 'he's a
dead man'. I knew I needed to take action.'

'What did you do?' I asked.

'Well, there was a big burly nurse shouting questions at me,' said John. 'She asked if I was allergic
to anything 'Yes, I replied.' The doctors and nurses stopped working as they waited for my reply. I
took a deep breath and yelled, 'Gravity"

Over their laughter, I told them, 'I am choosing to live.
Operate on me as if I am alive, not dead.'

He lived, thanks to the skill of his doctors, but also because of his amazing attitude... I learned
from him that every day we have the choice to live fully.

Attitude, after all, is everything.

Author Unknown

STRESSMASTER INTERNATIONAL

STRESSMASTERY ACTION PLAN

Stressmastery Action Plan*

Stress Symptom Checklist

Below are symptoms people experience when exposed to stress. If you have experienced a symptom in the past two weeks, rate the severity of discomfort from that symptom by entering a number next to that particular symptom using a scale of 1 to 5, with 1 being slight discomfort, 3 being moderate, and 5 being extreme discomfort. Under each symptom, write down your top 3 symptoms.

Physical Symptoms

___headaches
___indigestion
___stomach aches
___sweaty palms
___cold hands, feet
___dizziness
___easily fatigued
___muscle tension
___back pain
___tight neck, shoulders
___racing heart

___shallow breathing
___restlessness
___ringing in the ears
___constipation
___diarrhea

1. _____
2. _____
3. _____

Behavioral Symptoms

___excess smoking
___bossiness
___eating too little or too much
___critical attitude of others
___short-tempered
___procrastination
___sleeping too much or too little
___driving too fast
___grinding of teeth

___overuse of alcohol
___inability to finish tasks
___nail biting
___fidgety

1. _____
2. _____
3. _____

Emotional Symptoms

___bothered by unimportant things
___nervousness, anxiety
___boredom
___edginess
___irritable
___feeling "burned out"
___feeling powerless
___crying easily
___overwhelming pressure

___anger
___loneliness
___unhappiness, depression
___moodiness
___feeling helpless

1. _____
2. _____
3. _____

*Reprinted with permission from Dr. Laura Belsten.

STRESSMASTER INTERNATIONAL

Cognitive Symptoms

___loss of humor
___trouble thinking clearly
___being self-critical
___difficulty with concentration, focus
___being pessimistic
___forgetfulness
___lack of creativity
___expecting too much from others
___inability to make decisions
___constant worry

1. _____
2. _____
3. _____

Daily Stressors Worksheet

1. What are your stress triggers? What situations occur, on a regular basis, which cause you to feel stressed?

2. With which people are you likely to find yourself feeling stressed or tense?

3. How do you currently deal with stress?

4. What physical clues let you know you are feeling stressed?

5. Do you experience any behavioral changes when you are feeling stressed? If so, identify those here.

6. What do you feel emotionally in response to stress?

7. Complete the Stress Symptom Checklist. Which symptoms of stress are you most likely to notice first?

STRESSMASTER INTERNATIONAL

Action Plan & Commitment to Stress Mastery

Directions: Fill in the following spaces to create your own plan of action for when you return to work. With awareness comes responsibility – by becoming more aware you can make better decisions for yourself, your health, your family and your co-workers.

The stress symptoms I most need to notice and pay attention to are:

My stress triggers include the following (situations and people):

A better way to deal with each of these will be to (list the stress management techniques you will use here):

How will you remember to engage in stress management in the moment, at the onset of feeling stressed?

Stress Management and Stress Reduction Techniques

- Breathing exercises
- Progressive relaxation
- Visualization - (visualize yourself in a place that you find most relaxing and enjoyable)
- Listen to music and/or relaxation tapes (you can buy them or record your own)
- Refute irrational ideas (is what you just told yourself really true?)
- Various spiritual or religious practices (prayer, reflection, meditation, contemplation)
- Practice gratitude (and try to forgive)
- Avoid people and situations that cause stress (to the extent possible)
- Pare down your "to-do" list
- Call a good friend or find other ways to connect with others (share your feelings)
- Engage in realistic goal setting and time management
- Practice assertiveness and boundary setting (learn to say "no")
- Stop trying to control the uncontrollable
- Keep your sense of humor
- Practice good nutrition – eating a healthy diet makes us better prepared to cope with stress
- Get enough sleep
- Sweat the stress out through exercise (take a run or walk, stretch, do yoga, lift weights)
- Make time for fun and relaxation. Take a hot bath, get a massage, play with a pet, work in your garden, curl up with a good book, write in your journal, watch a comedy, spend time in nature.
- Nurturing yourself is a necessity, not a luxury – only you can take care of yourself – no one else can do this for you.
- Other ideas?

STRESSMASTER INTERNATIONAL

CONTRACT FOR CHANGE

The Contract For Change Form is your personal commitment to making a positive change toward STRESSMASTERY. Review the **Stress Warning Signs Section** and select ONE area to work on. By completing this contract you are agreeing that this area is in need of change and that you will do something about it.

STEP 1: Select the Risk Area to Work On - If you scored HIGH or MEDIUM on any of the Seven Stress Warning Signs Scales, it is recommended that you focus on the one area of greatest concern to you at this time. Other areas can be worked on, but it is better to make small changes in a critical area than to attempt to do too many things. The key to effective change is to get some initial positive results. STRESSMASTERY is a lifelong process for all of us. Be patient. Work hard. Results will follow.

STEP 2: Identify What You Will Change - Following are the behaviors, thoughts, or attitudes which I will change (be positive).
1. _____
2. _____
3. _____

STEP 3: What Will Stop or Prevent You From Being Successful - Some barriers are: other people, things, attitudes, lack of knowledge, lack of commitment, etc.
1. _____
2. _____

STEP 4: I Will do the Following to Overcome These Barriers:
1. _____
2. _____
3. _____

STEP 5: Assess Your Commitment:
My level of commitment to change is (circle one):   HIGH   MED   LOW

STEP 6: Time Allocation:
I will allow myself _____ months to achieve a reasonable level of success.

STEP 7: Commitment to Change:
I COMMIT to accomplish this goal! _____

**STEP 8: I will give Permission to_____ to help hold me accountable for this change.

IMPORTANT: Copy and share this contract with another person as soon as possible. Post on your refrigerator, bathroom mirror, or office wall! Let others help you to be accountable for your change. Remember, a secret goal is rarely achieved.

STRESSMASTER INTERNATIONAL

KEYS TO STRESSMASTERY

Ephesians 4:29 (NIV)
"Do not let any unwholesome talk come out of your mouths,
but only what is helpful for building others up according to their needs,
that it may benefit those who listen."

The Stress Response is a Choice. So, too, is the Relaxation Response! Choose the Relaxation Response...it works to bring your body, mind and spirt back into balance.

Life is a journey over which you have some control...even if you choose to do nothing to improve your life and reduce your stress, you have made that choice.

Stressmastery begins within changing your thinking, expectations and perceptions...not by trying to change the people and events around you.

Determine what you can and cannot change. Take action to affect a change when a change is possible. If the stressor cannot be changed–change your thinking about the stressor and "let it go".

Recognize that your actions and words can be the source of incredible stress to others and, even, yourself! Use the power of positive words and an upbeat attitude to affect a change in your world.

Fear and anxiety are at the root of many stress problems. Flow with fear of rejection, failure or not being in control. Fear is simply a function of how you perceive the threats of the world, even when the threat is only being a few minutes late. Flow and "let go"!

Keep expectations realistic. Nothing gets a person into trouble faster than expecting something that cannot or will not happen. If it isn't going to happen, change or lower your expectations. That's the choice. 90% of all the things we worry about never happen.

Use the resources available when you believe you have a problem. Work at problem solving, not playing the blame game. Seeking sympathy for your misfortunes will not change your misfortunes and will only hinder your movement toward stressmastery. If you are chronically depressed, seek out an appropriate doctor to see if your depression is influenced by stress or perhaps some chemical imbalance in your body.

Avoid over using chemical substances to control your anxious and stressful feelings. Exercise, deep relaxation, giving or receiving a massage, walking, or listening to music are far better at producing serenity and calm than any chemical. Plus, you remain in control of your life.

STRESSMASTER INTERNATIONAL

RESOURCES

For additional assistance on your road to **STRESSMASTERY**, consider one or more of the following:

1 If in a Crisis Call...

- 911
- EAP
- Information and Referral Service in your community
- A friend, spouse, minister or rabbi
- Your physician or mental health professional

2 If not in a crisis, but for rapid help contact one or more of the following:

- Local or Prov. Psychological Association Information and Referral
- Local or Prov. Social Worker's Association Information and Referral
- Your physician, hospital or clinic
- A psychologist, psychiatrist, marriage and family counselor or social worker
- A clergy member

3 World Wide Web

www.**Stressmaster**.com
www.nimh.gov .... National Institute of Mental Health
www.nih.gov .... National Institute of Health
www.medscape.com .... You may need to create a login I.D.
www.healthcentral.com ..... Good general health and mental health topics
www.intelihealth.com .... The John Hopkins Medical Newsletter

4 Recommended Resources

1. 100 Great Ideas to Relax & Reduce Stress, Wavering, Lila Empson (Editor), Tyndale Pub, 2010
2. Biblical Meditation For Spiritual Breakthrough, Towns Elmer, Regal Books, 1998
3. Contentment: The Secret To A Lasting Calm, Swenson Richard, NavPress, 2013
4. Conflict Management in Congregations, Editor – David B. Lott, Alban Institute, 2001
5. Dangerous Calling, Tripp Paul David, Crossway Pub, 2012
6. Five Dysfunctions of A Team, Lencioni Partrick, Josscy-Bass Pub, 2002
7. How Will You Measure Your Life, Clayton M. Christensen, James Allworth, Karen Dillon, (2012) Harper Collins Pub.
8. In Search of Balance, Swenson Richard, NavPress, 2010
9. Leading Change, Kotter, John P., Library of Congress, 1996
10. Leading On Empty, Cordeiro Wayne, Bethany House Pub, 2009
11. Margin: Restoring Margin to Overloaded Lives, Swenson Richard, NavPress, 2004
12. Meditation and Communion with God, Contemplating Scripture in an Age of Distraction, Davis, John Jefferson, IVP Academic Pub, 2012
12. Perilous Pursuits, Stowell Joseph M, Moody Press Pub, 1994
13. Simple Church, Rainer Thom, Rainer Eric, Broadman & Holman Pub, 2006
14. Success to Sinificance, Lloyd Reeb, Zondervan Pub, 2004
15. The Choice, Hoag Gary, Rodin Scott, Willmer Wesley, ECFA Press, 2014
16. The Peacemaker, Sande Ken, Baker Books Pub, 2004
17. The Overload Syndrome, Swenson Richard, NavPress, 1998
18. The Search for Significance, McGee Robert, Thomas Nelson Pub, 2003
19. The Winning Attitude, Maxwell John C, Thomas Nelson Pub, 1993
20. The Work of Leaders, Julie Straw, Mark Scullard, Susie Kukkonen, Barry Davis, Wiley Pub, 2013
21. Transitions: Leading Churches Through Change, Mosser David, Westminster John Know Press, 2011

5 To order additional copies of the SMQ-CMV...

Rev. Paul Bailey, MA
3C Training Solutions
32-54 St, Wasaga Beach, ON, L9Z 1W9
Ph. 705-607-1058
www.3c-coaching.com

"Turning Potential Into Performance"

www.ingramcontent.com/pod-product-compliance
Lightning Source LLC
Chambersburg PA
CBHW080745250426
43671CB00038B/2871